Get a Grip!
On a Heavenly Perspective…

How to keep a grasp on God's Perspective during these troubled times..

~

By Chris Louer

Copyright © 2008 by Chris Louer

Get a Grip! On a Heavenly Perspective…
How to keep a grasp on God's Perspective during these troubled times..
by Chris Louer

Printed in the United States of America

ISBN 978-1-60647-370-2

All rights reserved solely by the author. The author guarantees all contents are original and do not infringe upon the legal rights of any other person or work. No part of this book may be reproduced in any form without the permission of the author. The views expressed in this book are not necessarily those of the publisher.

Unless otherwise indicated, Bible quotations are taken from The New King James version{s} of the Bible. Copyright © 1997 by Thomas Nelson Publishers, Inc.

www.xulonpress.com

This book is dedicated to:

My beloved husband, Ron,
My beautiful daughters,
Missi & Adrianne,
My dear friends,
And my Aunt Estella,

Who loved me, supported me,
Prayed for me,
And made me laugh when I needed it…

Table of Contents

✱

Introduction ix

1. Losing our Grip..13
2. Single-Minded Boot camp; Are You Ready
   to Enlist? 19
3. Simply a Matter of Trust 27
4. Don't Look Now, but it Looks Pretty Ugly
   Down There! 33
5. Help! How Do I Untangle the mess?? 39
6. Sweet Surrender 45
7. My Ambition is to Please God.......................51
8. Dress up Right...61
9. A Dose of Thankfulness Can Cure Your Ills....67
10. My Heart is After Yours O'God 73
11. Choices that Make Winners! 79
12. Laughter Can be Good Medicine…................85

Introduction

Make no mistake. God has called you; *yes you* to live at this very time in this generation. If you have children and grandchildren, or great-grandchildren, they were also called to live in this generation as well. God has not left us as helpless orphans my friend in a dark world. Our Heavenly Father has given us His Holy spirit within us, and has sent His Son, Jesus Christ to be victorious at the cross on our behalf. As the world gets darker, our Father in heaven will extend His grace to us in greater measure to meet the need. God will always give His saints **what they need** for every generation until Jesus comes back! It's up to us to hold onto and use the valuable tools God has mapped out in His Word. It's **our choice** to apply what Jesus did on the cross to our personal situation.

Getting a grip on God's heavenly perspective doesn't just happen by itself. This world is going to give us many opportunities to encounter problems or situations that we feel we just can't handle. It's one thing to *want* God's perspective on a situation; it's another thing to go after it.

I wrote this book as a practical guide to help the child of God get a Godly perspective of how to ride these dark days as an overcomer instead of a defeated victim. I want to show how to use the tools God has given us to *Get a Grip* now so that we can move forward and accomplish in this life what God has called us to do.

Beloved Arise…

Yes, you were called to this time and place,
To serve and glorify God,
To raise your children and your grandchildren
In the teachings of our Lord~

The days may be dark,
But Jesus is Light,
And the Light dispels the darkness…

So, Arise my beloved and take your place,
In the army of the Lord.
Suit up in His armor and walk in His love,
Extend your hand in time of need,

Let Jesus find you as an overcomer,
When He returns again in lightning speed…
By Chris Louer

Isaiah 60:1-2 "Arise, shine, for your light has come! And the glory of the Lord is risen upon you, for behold the darkness shall cover the earth and deep darkness the people; but the Lord will arise over you and His glory will be seen upon you."

1

Losing Our Grip

✻

Losing our grip on a heavenly perspective is not hard to do, especially in this day and age. All of us at some point may find ourselves tangled in a web of anxiousness over strayed children, overburdened by financial concerns, or health issues. You may have suffered a loss in your life or your marriage may be in jeopardy. It may be a matter of just being too busy. Even ministry can cause us to lose our grip if we're not careful or maybe it's just a sense of feeling so alone in a lost world. Whatever the case may be, anxiousness can overtake us at times and that is why the bible addresses this very issue.

God knows the things that His children will face. He warns us of impending things to come and gives us guidelines to face these challenges as they come. *"But know this, that in the last days, perilous times will come. For men will be lovers of themselves, lovers of money, boasters, proud, blasphemers, disobedient to parents, unthankful, unholy, unloving, unforgiving, slanderers, without self control, brutal despisers of good, traitors, headstrong, haughty, lovers of pleasure rather than lovers of God…" 2 Timothy 3:1-4* All we have to do is turn on the five o'clock or six o'clock news to remind us that evil is rampant, and truly we are in the last days. Yet…when we hear these things, we seem surprised; as if God hadn't already warned us of it all. If this was all God had to say, we would have reason to lose our grip. However, God always gives encouragement, comfort and solutions to His solemn warnings. He has given us His Word so that we as His children would be thoroughly equipped as well as His Holy Spirit within us, to comfort, encourage, empower us, convict us of sin, teach us and guide us to do God's will. *"All scripture is given by inspiration of God and is profitable for doctrine, for reproof, correction, instruction in righteousness, that the man of God may <u>be thoroughly equipped</u> for every good work." 2 Timothy 3:16-17* God has anointed and given us the grace to be in exactly this generation and time period we are in. Walking in that anointing, however, means being single focused and abiding in Him. *"Abide in Me and I in you. As the branch cannot bear fruit of itself, neither can you unless you abide in me. I am the vine, you are the branches. He who abides in Me, and I in him, bears much fruit; for without Me you can do nothing." John 15:4-5* There it is…"*Without Me, you can do nothing.*" Apart from our single focus on Jesus, we will not have the anointing and grace to get us through these times. However, the word also says, *"If you abide in Me and My words abide in you, ask what you desire and it shall be done for you." John 15:17* The key is to abide in Him; not only on Sunday mornings, but every day. Sometimes it's a matter of literally climbing into that secret place where Christ is. *"He who dwells in that secret place of the most high, shall abide under the shadow of the Almighty. I will say of the Lord, He is my refuge and my fortress, My God; in Him I will trust." Psalm 91:1-2* Do we not have an awesome Father who has already made us citizens of a heavenly kingdom and we can actually dwell in that kingdom through Christ Jesus, and keep a heavenly perspective? That should give us something to be excited about!

If you are one who is struggling with keeping a heavenly perspective, or things look pretty muddy right now, be encouraged my friend. God's Word does have answers, and can bring clarity to an otherwise muddy situation.

Questions to Discuss

1. What is it specifically that concerns you the most during these end times?
2. Does it burden you at times? Read Matthew 11:28-30 What instruction does the scriptures give us when we are feeling overburdened?
3. How can you pray to relieve this burden?
4. What other scriptures can you find in God's Word that can comfort you or someone else during difficult times? Read 2 Corinthians 12:9, 2 Corinthians 1:1-5, 1Peter 5:8-11.
5. Read John 16:33 aloud. How does this scripture encourage us while living in these dark days?

Notes

2

Single-minded Boot Camp... Are you ready to Enlist?

✱

You can be a Christian for many years, and yet never truly experience the peace and joy of God. True, you will go to heaven someday, but anxiousness and discouragement will follow you if you do not learn the secret of being single-minded in the Lord. And believe me, this takes training! *"You therefore, must endure hardship as a good soldier of Jesus Christ. No one engaged in warfare entangles himself with the affairs of this life, that he may please him who enlisted him as a soldier."* **2 Timothy 2:3-4**

From the day we are born, the enemy is on a mission to pull you and me away from God and get us entangled in a web of this world, and get us discouraged. Unfortunately, he is often successful. This is why the bible so expressly warns us to guard our mind. *"If then you were raised with Christ, seek those things which are above, where Christ is, sitting at the right hand of God. Set your mind on things above, not on things on the earth. For you died, and your life is hidden with Christ in God." Colossians 3:1-3*

Learning to *set* our mind on things above is a choice and a discipline for sure. However, unless we learn that discipline as a soldier in Christ, we will never gain the victory in our lives we so desperately desire. Filling our mind with negative thoughts, and then entertaining those thoughts, is easy and very destructive. The enemy is always right there to feed our negative thoughts. Our own thought processes can be our greatest link to creative ideas or our greatest hindrance. Are the hands on your "thought clock" set more on negative thoughts or positive, constructive thoughts? I dare say, many people spend much of the hours in their day spent on negative thinking. It's no wonder we remain babies in Christ never moving from milk to meat, never reaching our full potential and purpose in God. It's not only others that may obstruct our path, but often our biggest obstacle in moving forward or taking risks for God is ourselves. "It'll never happen, I can't do this, someone else can do it so much better; why try and then fail? I really don't care to stretch myself anyway. I'd rather stay stagnant where it's comfortable", or is it?

That along with the determination of our own flesh to try to get control of our lives is a deadly combination, if not intercepted very quickly. The word says we need to *seek* those things which are above; those thoughts rarely come on their own. We need to always remember that the words *set* and *seek* are action words. Merely desiring to think the right thoughts is not enough. We must take action and learn to discipline our thoughts. To maintain a single-mind focus, the believer needs to keep it in Christ, or surely the world and negative thoughts will dominate. In the book of ***James, Chapter 1:8,*** the Word calls ***"a double-minded man unstable in all his ways."*** We know this certainly is not pleasing to the Lord, nor will it keep us mentally and spiritually healthy. On my regular *to do* list is to read ***Philippians 4:8*** aloud: ***"Finally, brethren, whatever things are true, whatever things are noble, whatever things are just, whatever things are pure, whatever things are lovely, whatever things are of good report, if there is any virtue and if there is anything praiseworthy, meditate on these things."*** Remember, life will always have its challenges, but as God's child, He has given us the right and the tools to experience His love, His joy and His peace.

Experiencing God's love, joy, and peace, did not come easily to me in my early years. Keeping my focus was difficult. Fear dominated my life, and where there is fear, there is not room for love, joy, or peace. Even married people with wonderful spouses can feel alone. I was one of those people. Did you know that even gentle and "nice" people can be "control freaks"? I wanted to control my environment to feel safe and not anxious. Even though I had a devoted husband, and on the outside seemed confident, on the inside I was suffering. New places, new employment, large groups that weren't structured, always made me feel anxious. I wasn't in control of what could happen. That frightened me terribly. So, I would just avoid social gatherings. Other than family and church, my life was pretty much indoors. Even though behaviors in my extended family could be rather neurotic, loud, and even combative at times, at least it was predictable. I became very reclusive which was not healthy or productive.

When you become reclusive, you move yourself away from situations where you can give and grow as a person. Friends and groups of people can balance you and offer accountability for you. Nothing can be more valuable than a "reality check" from a friend or reliable person at the right time. If you spend too much time alone; that may leave you with just *you* and *you*…a hazardous combination! We can become more introspective, insecure, and over all more complicated as a person. We can actually experience more physical ailments as well. The more we try to control our environment, the more we will shrink back as the person God created us to be and we become self absorbed. After all, it's safer to be alone than to be entangled with other people, right? Wrong! Remember this dear friend; Jesus is all about relationships; first his relationship with you and me. In general, God enjoys relationships with people, and that's where He places the most value… We are to follow His example. I am so grateful to God that he healed and restored me from my fears, as I allowed His love to come in and envelop me. It was when I implored God to help me that He met me.

God is always faithful. It was a process that would take several years. However, because of this healing, I was no longer afraid of groups, new people or situations in general. In fact, I found I genuinely enjoyed people and had a new found joy in life. You see, God had gifted me to teach and encourage others. Isn't it just like the enemy to try to hinder and cripple us in the very area we are most gifted?

Where is the enemy trying to cripple you? God is here now to meet you where you're at and heal you, if you allow Him to love you as only our Heavenly Father can.

Questions to Discuss

1. Read Colossians 3:1-3. What are some practical steps that you can take to "set" your mind on the "things above", when you are feeling negative or discouraged?
2. When someone you are talking with is in a "funk", do you join them and feed them more "funk" or do you try to find some way to first listen and then turn the conversation to a positive at the appropriate time?
3. Read Philippians 4:8 aloud. Either say or write down at least five good things you can meditate on and be grateful for this week.
4. Has there been a time in your life you have felt alone or isolated? How did you handle those feelings? How might you handle it differently now?
5. Where has the enemy tried to cripple you? (in the past or present) What steps did you take then or can you take now to overcome the fear and move forward?

Notes

3

Simply a matter of Trust
✱

Sometimes, we as God's child feel like children with empty hands; empty of the promises of God we so passionately want to cling to. This of course, is a lie, but a common feeling among the saints, and the enemy wastes no time in feeding this lie. Waiting on an answer from God is one of the hardest tasks we will face on this earth; especially when it concerns something or someone we feel passionate about. Believe me; our Father will give us many opportunities to practice waiting. Sometimes we hear…nothing. It's out of our hands; we can do nothing. ***Sometimes, it's simply a matter of trust***; having faith in a God who always promises to be faithful to you and me. Regardless of the time frame we might impose on him, God is never in a hurry. ***Hebrews 11:1 says, "Now Faith is the substance of things hoped for, the evidence of things not seen.***" There it is: faith is substance. It's very tangible, but in the Spirit. Faith is not just empty matter or a pipe dream. The bible says faith is substance and "...it's evidence of things not seen..." promises that have not yet manifested themselves, yet answers for our problems or evidence that we can hold onto while we wait. Always when we trust, it must be in Jesus Christ; not in our style of prayer, not in what we can do, but in Jesus Christ of Nazareth. He is where our faith must lye. After all, we are in His hands.

It seems so simple...just to trust in God. Then why do we try to make things so complicated as we wait? If for no other reason, we as children of God should trust God, simply because it pleases Him to have faith, and without faith the word says, we can't please Him. *"But without faith, it is impossible to please Him, for he who comes to God must believe that He is, and that He is a rewarder of those who diligently seek Him." Hebrews 11:6* The bible promises that He is a rewarder, a rewarder of those who believe in Him and seek Him.

So, a matter of trust is just that; it is matter, it is substance. God promises, *"We shall reap in due season, if we do not grow weary in well doing and lose heart." Galatians 6:9*

Waiting on God was no stranger to me. I went through the "waiting on God for the impossible" early on in my marriage, when my husband and I decided we wanted children. This was so natural, so easy, right? After all, God is the creator of all things; of course He would want us to have children. To top it off, my husband was one of those kinds of men who was very nurturing. He would make such a good father. We seemed to be the perfect couple to raise healthy, Godly children.

However, I had a problem. I could not seem to carry a baby past three months. I had no trouble getting pregnant, but when ten to twelve weeks rolled around, it was always the same. In a period of four years, I had six pregnancies. Five were miscarriages, and one was an ectopic pregnancy when I almost died. Where was God? I came to a place out of my despair that I had to simply trust God. There were no answers for me. From the ectopic pregnancy, it was determined that I had a very infected tube and enlarged ovary, which had to be removed surgically. That left me with one tube and one ovary. Remember, **"Nothing is impossible with God."** I still held onto hope that we would someday have children, but just didn't know how.

At my lowest point, after all the miscarriages, my Aunt Estella, (who I am very close to), sent me a letter and said she had had a dream. In this dream, I was pregnant with one child, while holding another infant on my lap. I can't tell you the encouragement I felt from that letter.

Three months later, I conceived, and on August 11, 1977, my first daughter, Melissa was born. Three years later, when I was eight months pregnant with my second daughter Adrianne, and was holding Melissa in my lap, I recalled my aunt's dream. My second beautiful daughter, Adrianne was born on July 31, 1980. Both pregnancies were healthy and with no complications. God is good!

Remember, faith is not empty. Faith in a living God who can and enjoys doing the impossible is substance! Trusting God means also accepting His timing to give you what you desire. Looking back, I realized our daughters were born just at the perfect time. Four years prior, I was still healing from fears and depression. Now I was in a better place to raise healthy children.

Maybe you're someone waiting on God for something. If its children remember, God has ways of answering prayers through adopting children as well. We never quite know what God's ultimate plan is – We just have to trust him…in all things.

Someday, when I go home to be with the Lord, I expect to see the children I had lost in miscarriages. What joy! I will be with them for eternity!

Questions to Discuss

1. Have you had to wait on God for something in your life?
2. Read Hebrew Chapter 11. As you read the "Hall of Faith", what do you see that these people had in common? What difficulties must they have faced while waiting in faith? Discuss two people that are listed in scripture.
3. What practical steps can we take when doubt begins to attack our mind regarding God's promises to us?
4. Read Hebrews 11:1 once again. Do you have a fresh perspective now in waiting on God for something?
5. Faith in God also means accepting His final decision concerning our requests to Him. Can you think of a time you believed in God for something and the outcome was different than you might have desired? How did you feel about this outcome, and what do you think is a Godly response from the child of God when God doesn't answer the way we think He should?

Notes

4

Don't Look Now, but it Looks Pretty Ugly Down There

✱

The heart is an amazing organ. On the one hand, it pumps blood that runs through our arteries to sustain life. It controls our mind, will and emotions. This amazing organ can also, on the other hand, seemingly betray us sometimes. It's unthinkable how ugly our thoughts, attitudes, and motives can be. "Did that attitude really come from me? I can't believe I just said that." Yes…we sometimes even shock ourselves with thoughts of envy, bad attitudes, a complaining spirit, willful disobedience, or judging others when surely we know how much grace God has granted to us. We can have self pity, an angry temper, indulging in unholy habits, or just be plain "bull-headed." Have I hit on anything you deal with yet or have dealt with in the past? Probably so…if we're really honest with ourselves. Being honest is not easy when you consider yourself a descent person or a mature Christian who desires to lead a holy life. It can feel downright embarrassing, not to mention mortifying to admit to yourself and worse to God, that a sin is rearing up its ugly head again in our lives. Not to mention how guilty we can feel and heartbroken over letting God down.

This may be a new revelation to you or maybe one you've forgotten. Our Father is not surprised at our sin and certainly not embarrassed by it. God *loves* you and me unconditionally, regardless of our sin. Yes, the word says the Holy Spirit does, and may grieve over our sin, but always convicts us leading us to repentance in Jesus Christ, to receive His forgiveness. This is all arranged by our Father in heaven, because of His great love for His children. You see, it's very difficult to hear from God or get His heavenly perspective, when our heart is plugged up with "gunk!" You know what I mean. All of us have arteries that have filled with "gunk" at times, that affect our heart condition. This can also affect our prayer life, and the back and forth communication from the Holy Spirit. How can we possibly hear from God when the lines are all clogged? The key to this is to readily confess our sin, so that the "gunk" is removed, giving us a healthy heart once again, and clean, clear, lines. ***Acts 3:19 says, "Repent, therefore and be converted, so that your sins may be blotted out, so that times of refreshing may come from the presence of the Lord."***

Merely admit to your trouble area. If for example, its stubbornness, ask God to forgive you for your stubbornness and then ask Him to give you a more flexible, teachable spirit. One that is willing to *listen* and consider other opinions besides your own. Ignoring your trouble area is not the answer. The problem will intensify as you get older if its not dealt with now. Acknowledge your sin; we all have sinned. Then ask God's forgiveness. He's there to meet you, forgive you, and refresh you.

Questions to discuss

1. Is there a particular area of sin that keeps reoccurring in your life?
2. Have you been honest about this sin to yourself? Have you confessed your sin to God to receive His forgiveness?
3. Read James 5:16 aloud. What does this verse instruct the believer to do if he or she is walking in sin? What are the benefits from confessing your sin to someone else?
4. Read aloud Acts 3:19 again. According to this verse, what is the benefit of repenting of our sin?
5. Read John 8:31-36. What do these verses say to the believer who thinks he might be a slave to sin?

Notes

5

Help! I'm Tangled up! How do I Untangle the Mess?

※

Have you ever cried *"help"* to God because you've gotten into a situation that seems out of control? Or maybe you made one or two unwise decisions or choices that have landed you in a mess. Whatever the case may be, most of us, (if we live long enough) will find ourselves in a puddle of mud that was either out of our control, or we brought it on ourselves by making a bad choice. Here's a newsflash: *bad choices lead to bad consequences.* Also, there are times in life when we find ourselves in a situation not made from a wrong choice, but because we are still living in a fallen world. Whatever the case may be, it can feel overwhelming to say the least. Often, there doesn't seem to be an answer or a solution; at least one we can think of. So what should we do when we find ourselves in this kind of situation?

First of all, know that God is a champion in bringing clarity to a seemingly muddy situation. After all, He sees all and knows all…He is God. He will give you as much information as He sees fit, not how much we think we should know. Also know, that God forgives and restores. That's what He does because of His great love for us. Next, God is for you and desires you to get back on track and He's there to help us. The word says He will strengthen you through the situation. ***Isaiah 41:10 "I am thy God; I will strengthen thee; yea, I will help thee; yea I will uphold thee with the right hand of My righteousness." Psalm 46:1 "God is our refuge and strength, a very present help in trouble."*** Remember too, that God works through our weakness. ***Isaiah 40:29 "He giveth power to the faint; and to them that have no might He increaseth strength…"***

So often when we are tangled in a mess, we want to undo the mess ourselves. True, we may or may not have made choices to get to this place, but once we're tangled up, *only God can help us to untangle the mess.* Somehow, we always think we can fix things on our own. Go to God and ask, "God help me… What should I do first?" I ask this question, because when one is in a mess, often there seems to be many loose ends; that's why we feel so overwhelmed. When we go to God and ask what you should do, first, it eliminates all the other loose ends for now and begins to bring some clarity and simplicity to the situation. True, you might have a long way to go in a total solution to the problem, but at least you have a beginning place. Go to God…*and listen.* You might not hear anything right away, but if you wait you will feel compelled to do something, or maybe compelled to do nothing for now. Whatever the case may be, you're on the right track. Ask God to forgive you for any part you've played in helping to create this mess, if any. As time goes on, the Holy Spirit will guide you step by step out of the problem. It may take some time. These things are not solved overnight, usually. If God chooses to allow you to continue to walk through a situation, He has a solution for that to: *His grace. 2 Corinthians 12:9 "My grace is sufficient for you, for My strength is made perfect in weakness."* In other words, God's strength will take over your strength. He will give you His strength and His grace. He will walk with you, through the turmoil, through the problem. What a comfort that should be to all of us. Also He provides comfort and rest to the weary heart. *"Come unto me all of you who labor and are heavy laden, and I will give you rest. Take My yoke upon you and learn from Me for I am gentle and lowly in heart, and you will find rest for your souls. For My yoke is easy and My burden is light." Matthew 11:28-30*

What an awesome God we serve! Even when we mess up or just cry out to Him, He's always there to embrace us. He will not turn us away, because that is not His nature. Our Father in heaven does not choose to give us what we deserve. His mercy and lovingkindness is unending. Ask God to show you your original commitment or plan, and where you veered off. Then ask God to help you get back on course. He's faithful and He'll help you.

Sometimes, however, in the process of restoration, God may not remove the consequences of our wrong choices; because of His love, and so we will learn. We still might have to endure the discipline of getting back on track. It may take some time before you get in that desired place, whatever that may be. What a blessing however, to know we're back in line with God, forgiven, and loved. Appreciate and absorb the richness of this time with God. Often when we are in a humbled state, and have to remain so close to our Father, we grow as a child of God. As you later look back, you will realize these were some of your richest times with the Lord.

Questions to Discuss

1. Is there an area in your life that has been difficult to untangle in your life?
2. Have you asked God to forgive you for your part of the problem? Have you asked Him to intervene in the situation even if you've done nothing wrong?
3. What is the *first step* that you can take to resolve this issue? (remember, just one) After you've taken that first step, God will show you the next step.
4. Do you have a trusted friend or counselor you can share this with, pray with you and be accountable to?
5. Remember to thank God in advance for His intervention and willingness to help you get back on track. Keep thanking Him all the way through the process. Read Philippians 4:6-7. Read these scriptures aloud and put your name in as you read it. Does that help to make it more personal to you? After reading this scripture, what are the rewards that come from following the instructions in verse 6?

Notes

6

Sweet Surrender

✽

Nothing will cause you to have a heavenly perspective faster than to surrender – surrendering to Jesus. Remember, Jesus Christ must be Lord of your life every day. If you are not surrendered to Jesus Christ, ***something else will*** become lord of your life, make no mistake. This will cause you to lose all perspective of what God is doing and we will be swallowed up by our problems.

I start every time of morning prayer with ***"Jesus Christ, you are Lord of my life. I surrender to you today."*** I actually say it aloud. It sounds so simple and yet it's very powerful. Just the simple act of speaking this out, reminds me who is to be in charge of my life today. It also puts the enemy on alert, that Jesus is my Lord, and I'll not bow to anything or anybody that the enemy puts in front of me.

Every day will be a new day that the world will fight to take lordship over my life and yours, in some way. Therefore, I acknowledge Christ's Lordship over my life each day. I need to surrender again every day, because each day will provide a new opportunity for the world to capture my eye or heart and rebel against God. *"**Therefore submit to God. Resist the devil and he will flee from you. Draw near to God and He will draw near to you...Humble yourselves in the sight of the Lord and He will lift you up."** James 4:7-10*

Asking Jesus to come into my heart, so that I may have eternal life with Him, and actually making Jesus Lord over my life were two separate events for me. I asked Jesus to come into my heart at the young age of seven. My mother and I had gone to visit my Aunt Estella one summer, (which by the way, I do not advise to do – July in El Paso, Texas is brutally hot!!). However, I was soon to find out July in Texas was not the only thing that was hot! There was a small group of ladies; that's all it was. My aunt had asked my mother and me to join her at a friend's home for a prayer meeting. And what a prayer meeting it was! There was a group of ladies holding hands and speaking softly in the living room of her home. Then, they started singing songs and clapping their hands. To be honest, at the time, I didn't know who or why they were singing at all. It all seemed so strange to me. My aunt introduced me to the group and before I knew it they were all praying over me. I didn't know why, but I felt oddly peaceful. My aunt proceeded to tell me the gospel message and asked me if I would like to ask Jesus into my heart. I said, "Yes" of course. Funny, as a child, everything seemed so simple, which really must have been so beautiful to the Lord and also for the women in the bible study.

My mother and I flew back to California at the end of that week. My mother had not yet accepted Christ. I was now the only Christian in our home. Something powerful definitely had happened that day. Being only seven years old, I didn't realize the full impact of that decision until sometime later. Oh yes...Did I mention that I lived in a home where there was constant yelling in our home, and going out at night and searching bars to find my dad? This was not an uncommon occurrence. My dad was an alcoholic. He was not abusive to me in the physical sense and most of his drinking was done out of the house. He preferred to go on 2-4 day "binges" which almost put my mother over the edge with worry over his safety. I could never count on my dad for my protection, stability, or just being there for me. He was truly wrapped up in his own world. In spite of his behavior, I loved him very much. My faith in God got me through those times.

Despite all the turmoil, I always had a very close relationship with my mother. She never put my father down; neither did she ever make excuses for his behavior. She truly handled a very difficult problem to say the least, with unusual wisdom I think. I was always encouraged to vocalize my feelings. She learned much take-home advice from a group called Allinon, for the spouses of alcoholics, and of course God. Much later, my mother realized just how much the Lord had intervened even before she became a Christian. My mother, at about 45 years of age, and my dad much later at 70 years, both accepted Jesus as their Savior. My Dad also stopped drinking and began attending church with my mother. Miracles do happen. ***"With men this is impossible, but with God, all things are possible!" Matthew 19:26.*** After my mother passed away, I experienced the joy of a father-daughter relationship. Those few years taking care of my father, were rich and very memorable ones for me, and I thank God for them.

Questions to Discuss

1. What area of your life do you need to surrender today?
2. What tactic does the enemy use to try to lure you into taking the problem back?
3. What steps do you think you can take to help you stay on track, surrendered to the Lord?
4. Why is surrender to the Lord so important in our lives? Why is relinquishing our control so difficult sometimes?
5. Read James 4:7. Note that *"submit to God"* and *"resist the devil"* are in the same verse. Why do you think we need to submit to God first for the enemy to flee?

Notes

7
My Ambition is to Please God
✳

In this day and age, especially in the United States, people seem to have plenty of ambition. Even among many Christians, the idea of American success lies in how many things you can acquire and how much money you make.

Ultimately, however, true ambition, according to God's Word, lies in pleasing God. *"But we have been approved by God to be entrusted with the gospel, even so we speak, not as <u>pleasing</u> men, but <u>God</u> who tests our hearts." 1 Thessalonians 2:4. "And whatever we ask we receive from Him, because we keep His commandments and do those things that <u>are</u> <u>pleasing in His sight." 1 John 3:22*

Our ambition must be to first please God. All other so-called successes and ventures are futile and will not receive eternal rewards, if God has not directed them. Misguided Christians can believe that every ministry or act of service to God must be accomplished by only them to be in God's will. However, only those plans truly directed by God for your life will please God and will receive eternal rewards. Again, our ambition must be to please God, not man, not ourselves.

Remember, to please God, our first ambition must be to nurture our walk with God. Next, we need to take care of and nurture our marriage partner, and nurture and disciple the children God has entrusted to us. Lastly, but very importantly, we must take care of the friendships God has given us. Nothing else can be fruitful if these priorities are neglected. Remember that God is primarily in the relationship business. The enemy's goal on the other hand, is to *divide* our relationships: with God, our spouse, our children, our friends, or with other people God has put in our life. God does not set us up for failure in our relationships when He calls us to ministry. On the contrary, we, above all, should be examples to others of a solid marriage and family, and strong friendships. This is healthy and pleasing to God. If you don't take care of these relationships now, they will return later to "slap you in the face" which can be very painful. By the way, if this does happen, know that our Father is ready to forgive and restore broken relationships, and you will have solid wisdom to hand out to others from first hand experience. Take care of your priorities first and you will then be free of relationship worries, and will be more effectively able to serve the Lord. If your ministry is taking up too much time away from your family, it's time to re-evaluate and clean off your plate; you've probably taken on too much. God only calls us to take on certain tasks; not all the tasks!

Keep in mind, that even seemingly mundane, menial or messy tasks, are anything but menial, if directed by the Lord. Taking care of small children, or an aged or ill parent may be all you can handle on your plate right now. However, God considers these things no less important than heading up a large ministry. Sometimes I think we will all be surprised at the eternal rewards that silent givers and servants behind closed doors will receive. The value we place on various tasks are much different than how our Heavenly Father sees it.

It's all about pleasing God; obeying Him, and the heart with which we do it. God is not impressed with showy ventures that have nothing to do with Him. Remember too, that part of pleasing God is obeying Him; even when it's difficult and you don't understand why He's calling you to do this. In this world of open rebellion and defiance, obedience seems like a new concept, but not to God, God has always required obedience from His children. This obedience pleases God and protects us. Of course, He is always there to welcome us back when we disobey or go our own direction.

Recently, I had that very challenge put before me, when my husband informed me that he felt we should give his dad, my father-in-law, an 85th birthday party. Now this may all sound very nice and a great idea from an outside party, who doesn't know all the history in this colorful man's life. How wonderful…an 85th birthday party to celebrate a member of our family's

Get a Grip! On a Heavenly Perspective...

life, who means so much to all of us; who has devoted his life to his dear wife and family...right? Wrong! Nothing could be further from the truth. Needless to say, without going into any detail, he was not a very good husband to my mother-in-law. I suppose he treated her the way his mother was treated by his Dad. To him that was normal and right. She was a dear woman who loved God and passed away about five years ago. After that, it was an endless cycle of phone calls and problems for my husband's dad who to our knowledge had never accepted Jesus Christ into his life. My husband did witness to him, however we never were really sure he got it; I suppose only God knows that answer, since he's the only one who truly knows the heart of a man. He insisted on making one bad decision after another, until finally, my husband took over his finances, (which Grandpa did not want to give up for sure...), and paid all his dad's bills. Because of his bad temper, he was alienated from the rest of the family. My husband and sister were the only ones who regularly went to visit him and made sure he was taken care of. After all, we were the Christians in the family. So, why would we want to give him a big birthday party? After all, my dear mother-in-law never had a big party.

As you can already probably hear in my attitude, I wasn't crazy about the idea of giving this party, and it was to be at our house as well! Why hadn't my husband talked to me about this first, before making the decision to tell his dad about this? We always talked about every major decision together...And believe me this was considered in the ***major*** category. Who would come to the party anyway, when everyone in the family was angry with Grandpa?

It didn't take long before God spoke to me about my husband's decision. First, he was my husband, and if this was so important to him to do this, knowing what he knew about his Dad, maybe this wasn't a bad idea after all. Maybe, could it be it was God putting this together? It couldn't be, I thought to myself. Nothing added up. His dad certainly didn't deserve this party. I knew it wasn't going to be any fun because everyone attending would come in a bad mood because they really didn't want to be there. But my husband really wanted this party, so I went to God and prayed to change my attitude.

It was in that prayer time God spoke to me about obedience to Him, even though I didn't understand it. He spoke to me about his forgiveness and grace and great love. He reminded me of all the times I received blessings I didn't really deserve because of my own sin. And the grace that was extended to me so many times. He spoke to me about the all encompassing love He has, even for the difficult people; a love we'll never completely understand until we see Jesus face to face in heaven someday. He spoke to me that this party would be so much more than merely a birthday party. The Father said He was going to do His business there, whatever that meant. It was in that moment that I realized this wasn't about the party or my father-in-law. This was about me and ***my obedience to my Father.*** In obeying and doing what my husband asked, I was obeying God.

Once I agreed in my heart to do this with a good attitude, I had to start praying; praying for family members to attend; praying for the Holy Spirit to be present and do His work among our family, and praying that when he went to pick up his dad, he'd be home! That's right...my husband drove all the way to Hemet and his dad wasn't there...just perfect...now he couldn't even find the birthday boy! My husband proceeded to drive to all of Grandpa's known hangouts. Finally, he found him casually talking to a friend at the local mall. "What was wrong?" Grandpa asked.

My husband eventually brought his dad to his sister's house where he waited until we were set up at our house, and the guests had arrived. Oh yes...did I mention that we got calls up until the last minute, of family members refusing to come to the party? I just kept praying...

The party turned out to be a total success. Every family member attended except two, so there was a large group to greet him. Everyone who attended, came with a wonderful attitude. It was truly supernatural! Our home was filled with laughter, and above all the loving presence of the Lord. Old family members got to get re-acquainted, and meet grandchildren and nieces and nephews they had never met before. Christians in the family were making connections with the non-Christians and setting up dinner dates. It was truly a miracle what God did at that party.

You see, God sees the whole picture...He *is* the heavenly perspective. We can never hope to understand it all on this earth, but someday we will when we are with our Lord Jesus Christ in eternity. In the meantime, we're doing good if we can keep a tight grip on His heavenly perspective.

Questions to Discuss

1. Do you think our ambition for ourselves might be different than God's ambition for us at times? What do you think helps to influence those desires?
2. Is there an area of your life God has called you to be obedient and it's difficult for you to obey? What's holding you back?
3. Acknowledge small ways or kindnesses in your life you have extended yourself to others in order to be obedient to God. Write them down. Look back at them when you feel discouraged and do not feel fruitful.
4. Do you believe our Father in heaven regards these acts as important as other acts you might see as more important? Ask God to give you His perspective on even the menial tasks you perform on a daily basis. I think you might be surprised.
5. Are there more ways you can be obedient to God where you've held back?
6. Acknowledge these areas to God, ask His forgiveness for your disobedience and ask for His help to take steps forward to accomplish what He has called you to do.

Notes

8

Dress Up Right

✻

Every day when you and I go out into the world, we can potentially face a battle; sometimes the battle is visible, but most of the time the battles are unseen. We must be in the proper attire at all times as a soldier who enters into battle, because whether you realize it or not, the battle is raging.

Clothe yourself in Jesus each morning. Put your armor on according to ***Ephesians Chapter 6*** in God's Word. This is something the child of God must do. We can be taught this, but at some point, ***Ephesians 6:11 says, "Put on the whole armor of God."*** We must do this ourselves. We must dress ourselves daily. Just as surely as we put our dress or shirt and pants on each day, we must clothe ourselves in Jesus and be armed.

To be fully clothed each day, we must develop a regular prayer life. We become clothed in Christ by being in His presence on a daily basis. To be like

Him, we must spend time with him, *before* we go out into the world. The word says in *Matthew 26:41, "Watch and pray, lest you enter into temptation; the spirit is willing but the flesh is weak."* God exhorts us to pray and the Holy Spirit will help us to resist temptations that will come our way.

Psalm 55:17 says, "Evening and morning and at noon will I pray and cry aloud and He shall hear my voice." Ephesians 6:18 says, "Praying always with all prayer and supplication in the spirit…"

The word also says to shed anxiousness and receive peace over a situation, when we pray. *Philippians 4:6-7 "Be anxious for nothing but in everything by prayer and supplication with thanksgiving let your requests be made known to God and the peace of God which passes all understanding will guard your hearts and minds in Christ Jesus."*

I begin my day with prayer in our bedroom on my knees. Find your own quiet place where you won't be interrupted. (If you're a mom with young children, it may be the bathroom!) Getting on my knees is a visible expression of surrender to Jesus as my Lord. For me, it gives Him the honor and glory He is so deserving of. I am giving Him my full attention and I am aware of His presence. My prayer time may only last 20 minutes at times; sometimes it's longer. At that time I begin by praising Him for who He is. (Reading one of the Psalms out loud is a great way to start…). Next, I recall all the wonderful blessings He has given me. I usually follow this by asking forgiveness for any unconfessed sin in my life. I then proceed to pray for my family, our President, our church and our pastor, and other people and situations God puts on my heart. Believe it or not, you can cover much in 20 minutes of uninterrupted prayer. I end by listening to hear what *God may say to me*. You may be surprised at the scripture He may give you to think about, or the thought He speaks to you. I then continue to talk to God all during the day as I take on the daily activities of life.

A prayer life is continuous communication with the Father, all during the day and sometimes the nighttime. Nothing, however, replaces the quiet, one on one time I have with God in the morning on my knees. These times with my Heavenly Father are uninterrupted and are rich.

If you are a young mother or dad with children or have a very hectic schedule, begin with just ten minutes each morning before babies wake up or work begins. Remember, God is not watching the clock. He is not impressed by time spent in prayer. He is drawn to you by your obedience and heart's desire to meet Him each morning before your day begins. He will meet with you in those 10 minutes, clothe you, and have you ready to meet the day.

Now let's get one thing straight…A prayer life is wonderful but without regular reading of God's Word, you will not grow as a Christian. It's as simple as that. To be transformed into a mature Christian, our mind must be renewed in Christ by reading God's Word. A child of God that grows and blossoms and bears fruit for the Lord, must be reading God's Word on a regular basis. ***Romans 12:2 "And do not be conformed to this world, but be <u>transformed by the</u>***

renewing of your mind*, that you may probe what is the good and acceptable will of God."*

There it is…Merely think of someone you admire who has a mature walk with God and I will show you a person who knows how to "dress up right". That is, they spend regular time with God in prayer and in His Word, so that they are clothed in Jesus *before* they walk out their door. When you dress up right, you are more apt to open your mouth in love and in words of wisdom You are more able to avoid pitfalls instead of falling into them. You also put the enemy on alert! Don't mess with me. I'm armed! That's something to shout about!

Questions to Discuss

1. Read *Ephesians 6:11-18*. Is there a regular time you can sit to read the Word each day? Ask God to help you commit to that time. Ask Him to speak to you as you read scripture.
2. Can you set a regular time of prayer each day with your Heavenly Father? What do you think the benefits will be?
3. What tends to interfere with committing to times of prayer and reading God's Word?
4. What are some practical steps you can take to stay with your commitment to praying and read God's Word?
5. Why is a regular prayer time and reading of God's Word important for the believer; especially during these times?

Notes

9

A Dose of Thankfulness Can Cure Your Ills

*

Remember the well known musical, Mary Poppins, when Mary is attempting to create a good attitude in the children as she is preparing to leave the household? She sang a song to them called, ***"Just a spoonful of Sugar Helps the Medicine go Down".*** In that scene, Mary knew a valuable secret. She knew if she could change the children's attitude from a negative to a positive attitude, Mary's departure from the household would go more smoothly and the children would focus on all they had gained instead of their loss. Also, they would hold onto valuable lessons that would enhance their future years.

Our Father knows His children. He knows our nature and its pitfalls. Our Father knows a thankful heart is crucial for the child of God to be able to endure the trials that would come our way, and maintain a healthy, emotional outlook on life. Just to live each day in this fallen world, a thankful heart is good medicine for a haughty, cynical, negative or depressing attitude, which can so easily overtake us at times.

A thankful heart also glorifies and gives praise that is due to a God who loves us, protects us, sustains us, provides for us, heals us, and who is absolutely and unequivocally worthy of our praise and thanks. If you can only be thankful for one thing, recall the great sacrifice our Father made for us in sacrificing His only Son, Jesus Christ, so that you and I would have eternal life with Him! That alone is worth pondering and thanking God for.

This is why our Heavenly Father offers numerous scriptures on just that subject: *giving thanks*. Do you recall the story of the ten lepers recorded in ***Luke 17:11-19***? Ten men who were lepers approached Jesus as He was traveling through Samaria and Galilee. They each cried for Jesus to have mercy on them for they were lepers who were not only very sick but were outcasts in their community. Jesus did have mercy on them and healed all ten lepers. Out of the ten, only one returned to say, **"*Thank you*"**. Think of it…Men who were previously shunned, looked down upon, and lived a life of isolation and suffering, were now suddenly healed! I think in their exuberance of being healthy again, they merely bypassed thanking the healer. What would you have done? Would you have taken the time to come back to thank the one who healed and restored your life? Yet, in verses 17 & 18, Jesus records these words, **"*Were there not*

ten cleansed? But where are the other nine? Were there not any found who returned to give glory to God but this foreigner?" This shows us Jesus not only acknowledges the one who came back to give thanks, but was saddened by the nine who didn't.

Yes, our Father desires His children to have thankful hearts. In fact, in ***1 Thessalonians 5:18***, He states that ***the giving of thanks*** is His will. ***"In everything give thanks, for this is the will of God for you.."***

A thankful heart will also create a peaceful state of mind. Notice the verse in the book of ***Philippians 4:6-7, "Be anxious for nothing, but in everything by prayer and supplication, with thanksgiving, let your requests be made known to God. And the peace of God which surpasses all understanding, will guard your hearts and minds in Christ Jesus."*** Being thankful brings peace.

No matter what you may be facing, you can always find something to be thankful for. In a difficult situation, find any small thing you can be thankful for and always acknowledge our Heavenly Father for these blessings; however small they may seem to you. This will keep your heart in the right place and it pleases God. A person with a thankful heart continues to find and acknowledge ways that God has blessed him or her even in the smallest ways. One with a thankful heart will ***seek*** to find reasons to thank God!

Here are some verses to ponder and recite aloud to give thanks to our Heavenly Father:

Psalm 95:1-3 "Oh come let us sing to the Lord! Let us shout joyfully to the rock of our salvation. Let us come before His presence with thanksgiving. Let us shout joyfully to Him with psalms. For the Lord is the great God, and the great king above all gods."

2 Corinthians 9:15 "Thanks be to God for His Indescribable gift!"

Ephesians 5:19-20 "Speaking to one another in psalms and hymns and spiritual songs, singing and making melody in your heart to the Lord. <u>Giving thanks</u> always for all things to God the Father in the name of our Lord Jesus Christ."

Psalm 50:14 "Offer to God thanksgiving, and pay your vow to the Most High."

Remember dear friends, the giving of thanks to a heavenly Father who is so deserving of our praise is not a request, it is a command. It's not if we feel like it, not only when something good happens in our life. We are to give thanks in all things and in all circumstances, for this is the will of God…

Questions to Discuss

1. What are some areas in your life you can thank God for?
2. Do you thank God for something He has done in your life every day?
3. Why is a thankful heart so important? How does a thankful heart spill into your life in other positive ways?
4. Think of a difficult situation you are facing now or have faced in the past. What is at least one thing you can thank God for in the situation?
5. Having read this chapter, when you are feeling depressed or discouraged, what do you think might be a positive step in pulling out of this state of mind?

Notes

10

My Heart is After Yours O'God

※

As I have already mentioned in a previous chapter, the heart is an amazing organ, and the bible has much to say about it. God has created us to have within us not merely a pumping organ, but an organ that is central to our very life. It pumps blood to the brain which allows our inner control panel to work. It affects how we think, what we say, our emotions, our actions, our ability to receive and sort information, and our conscience. This is why the Word so adamantly addresses the importance of our heart condition. *Proverbs 4:20-23 amplified, states, "My son attend to my words, consent and submit to my sayings. Let them not depart from your sight. Keep them in the center of your heart. For they are life to those who find them; healing and health to all their flesh. Keep our heart with all vigilance and above all that you guard it, for out of it flows the springs of life."*

David, in the Bible, was a man after God's own heart. God saw something very special in David. So, in 1 Samuel 16, God tells the prophet Samuel, He has chosen young David to be the new king. You see, David's peers, not even Samuel, could see David's potential; but God saw David's heart and so instructed Samuel to anoint David as king. ***1 Samuel 16:7 "But the Lord said to Samuel, "Do not look at this physical stature because I have refused him. For the Lord does not see as man sees. For a man looks at the outward appearance but the Lord looks at the heart". 1 Samuel 16:13. "Then Samuel took the horn of oil and anointed him in the midst of his brothers, and the Spirit of the Lord came upon David from that day forward. So David arose and went to Ramah."***

David knew that he needed to keep his heart clean before God. And know this – David by no means led a perfect life. Nothing could be farther from the truth. David made some grave errors in judgment which brought huge consequences along with it. But David was always repentant and sought God's forgiveness. David cries out to God in *Psalm 51:10* and says, *"Create in me a clean heart O'God and renew a steadfast spirit within me."* To remain strong and stable in the Lord, we need to go before God daily and ask Him to cleanse our heart from any impurities that might displease God and hinder our walk with Him. Always remember dear ones, that our Heavenly Father's love for us never changes or diminishes toward us even if our heart condition is sour. His love is unconditional. However, our close relationship and prayer life can be affected when our heart is impure. Our unclean heart will also pollute our thoughts, our words, and our actions. *"Create in me a clean heart O'God and renew a right spirit in me today."* This should be our prayer each and every day.

Remember also, that God desires us to praise, honor and love Him with our whole heart; not a divided heart. *Psalm 111:1 says, "I will praise the Lord with my whole heart in the assembly of the upright and in the congregation."*

I love to praise the Lord by reading the psalms aloud. *Psalm 28:6-7, declares "Blessed be the Lord, because He has heard the voice of my supplications. The Lord is my strength and my shield, my heart trusts in Him, and I am helped. Therefore, my heart greatly rejoices and with my song will I praise Him!" Hallelujah!*

Questions to Discuss

1. Read again 1 Samuel 16:7. How is our society so different today than God's view of the appearance of a man or woman?
2. After reading 1 Samuel 16, what should that tell the believer what Jesus looks for when calling someone to the ministry?
3. Why is it so important to monitor what goes into heart? How do you think our heart condition affects our behavior?
4. Do you think inappropriate movies, websites, TV shows, or reading material can affect us in an adverse way? Why?
5. How can a believer have a "divided heart"? Have you ever experienced this? What can we do to get back on track?

Notes

11

Choices That Make Winners
*

Life is full of choices. Like it or not, much of where we are today is because of choices we have made along the way to get to this place in our lives. We don't like to admit that sometimes, but it's true just the same.

Here is the good news. God is working on you and I on a daily basis encouraging us, guiding us, supporting us, cheering us on to become the winners He has created us to be. Regardless of past poor choices, God is a God of today. From here on out, He wants you and me to be the women and men He has called us to be. It's your decision, however, to get a grip and apply these ingredients to your life situation now! **Your choice**...just like it was your choice to invite Jesus into your heart and life.

You may be in the process right now of overcoming a problem area in your life. My weakness was fear. At some point, you have to make the decision to move forward in spite of the obstacles. I had to make the choice to move forward past my fears to obey God. Speaking in front of people to teach at retreats or conferences at first was terrifying to me. But at some point, my desire to obey and serve God was greater than my fear. It was at those times God met me and was faithful to accomplish what I needed to do. It was a choice I will never regret.

Without these important choices, you might never accomplish the purpose you are called to do. Life changes come from applying what Jesus did on the cross to your situation. Even though Jesus was victorious over all principalities and powers of darkness, there are still powers of darkness around us trying to tempt us, thwart us, battle against us, or discourage us! The battle won't end until we're taken up with our Lord in heaven.

Sometimes, life brings a problem to your doorstep that you hadn't invited, hadn't counted on, and certainly didn't choose. But there it is; knocking at your door. It may be a very difficult spouse, a wayward child, an unexpected illness, physical or emotional, financial crisis, or an aging parent. Whatever the case may be, the problem doesn't care that it's intruding on your life. It still walks right in. How does the child of God deal with troubles past or present that they did not choose? You are not helpless beloved! ***You can choose how you respond to the situation.*** Once you get over the shock of this problem daring to walk in your door, it's time to deal with it. Cowering in fear, instead of faith, or wallowing in self pity, will not make the problem go away. In fact, it's at these times you risk sinking down right along with the problem, and this dear ones is what the enemy desires. Instead, face the problem head on. Get prayer and council from a trusted friend or counselor. Ask God to give you wisdom to get through this situation, and to make wise decisions. Your Heavenly Father is there to help you. God will extend the grace you need to not only survive but overcome! ***"My grace is sufficient for you, for My strength is made perfect in weakness." 2 Corinthians 12:9***

Jesus was victorious at the cross! He gave us His Holy Word to stand on, and His Holy Spirit to lead us into all truth, comfort us, convict us, give us strength to resist temptations that will come our way, as well as guide us and teach us. He certainly has not left us helpless! Do not let anyone convince you dear ones that we don't have enough power in Christ to live in this fallen world. God will give His saints **what they need** for every generation until Jesus comes back again. You don't have to be anxious about your children, or your grandchildren's welfare. Just do your part to teach them about Jesus and God's Word and they will be more than survivors...they will be overcomers!

It's our choice to apply what Jesus did on the cross to our personal situation. Do you choose now to apply what you have learned to your life? You make the choice – God will make the changes within you. He will help you to rise up and receive His heavenly perspective!

Questions to Discuss

1. Are you anxious at times about your children or grandchildren's welfare? What have you learned or have been reminded of by reading this chapter?
2. Have you asked God's forgiveness for past poor choices?
3. Have you forgiven yourself and left it in your past, or do you continually put yourself down by reminding yourself of past poor decisions?
4. How do you think God feels when we fail to forgive ourselves? How can this hold us back from future success?
5. What is one choice or decision you can make today that has been a difficult one for you to make?

Notes

12

Laughter Can be good Medicine

✻

The word *"laugh"* in the [a]Websters Dictionary, is defined as to show mirth, joy, to find amusement in something with a smile, and a chuckle or explosive sound. Yes, our Heavenly Father, the God of this universe has created us with the ability to take pleasure, find amusement or yes just laugh out loud to certain life situations.

Having a sense of humor in this day and age can go a long way. Learning to take ourselves less seriously and be able to laugh at ourselves at times, is a healthy response at the appropriate time. It's a result of a lighthearted spirit, which we as children of God can truly benefit from and is precious to God. Don't you take pleasure when you hear your children laugh?

When I got married to my husband Ron at the age of twenty-one, I admit I was a pretty intense person. Yes, I was thoughtful; I think sensitive to my husband's needs, but I had a tendency to take other people, people's comments, and myself much too seriously. This was probably a result of my own childhood which was also pretty intense at times. I was famous for running dialogues of conversations through my head that I had had that day. Did I say the right thing? What did he or she mean by that? Yikes! That takes so much work!

God's remedy for me was to marry a man like my husband, who has a great sense of humor. He has the ability to laugh at himself and find humor in everyday situations. Over the years, laughter has gotten my husband and I through many difficult times. Some, we were not able to laugh at until years later, but when we recall those times, we still have a good chuckle. Once when we were at a restaurant, my husband and I began laughing over a situation at dinner. The server came up to us and said, "That's so nice you can still laugh together – You look like you really enjoy each other." That's pretty good, I guess, for thirty –five years of marriage. The point is, laughter came much easier for me over the years. I'm convinced more people would want to become Christians, if we didn't look so sour and serious all the time. We as Christians should be examples of having the most fun and enjoyment in life…

Even in bible times there were occasions that just had to make you laugh. One such instance of this is recorded in *Genesis 21:1-7.* Abraham and Sarah had been childless for many years. In those days, especially, being unable to have children was almost like a curse. Bearing children was a woman's greatest purpose in life. Sarah suffered much grief and ridicule during those waiting years, and made some poor decisions along the way. In spite of this, God finally did bless Abraham and Sarah with a son, Isaac. Sarah was well past childbearing years, and Abraham was 100 years of age! Think of it. How unlikely is this? No wonder in verses 6-7, Sarah said, ***"God has made me laugh and all who hear will laugh with me. Who would have said to Abraham that Sarah would nurse children? For I have born him a son in his old age."***

You see, often when the pain of a circumstance is over, we are blessed with a circumstance that brings joy. It was laughter that got my husband and I through some very difficult times. Early on in our marriage, we went through financial difficulties. We had two daughters to raise. My husband worked very hard in construction, but the work was sometimes sporadic. I was a stay at home mother at the time, as our children were young. When we look back now, we're amazed how we lived on the yearly income that we were receiving. I know it was God's provision that got us through those times and dear friends who helped out. At the time, it didn't seem funny at all, but as we look back we can recall some very funny situations.

One such time was years ago when we owned a Buick that was truly a "nightmare" The term "lemon" was too good to describe that car. My husband told me he frequently had visions of driving the car over a cliff, and jumping out and watching it crash and break into thousands of pieces. Those of you who've had such a car I'm sure can relate. We always had that car in the repair shop. Finally, it was decided we would trade in the car for another used car. Since we wanted to be honest in saying we had replaced just about everything on the car (which we had done and the receipts to prove it..), we had one last needed repair done; a new starter. Now we felt ready to "unload" this car on someone else.

We drove to the local car dealership near our home, drove into the parking lot, right up to the tall windows that showcase all the new cars and parked. A salesman promptly came out and we told him we were interested in purchasing a car and trading in this car which was in good running condition. It was a slow day so we had several onlookers and salesmen around us. What great service and attention we thought! My husband proceeded to get out of our car and explained to the salesmen from front to back all we had done to the car. "Even a new starter was just put in." my husband said. The salesman seemed impressed until he asked my husband to please move the car over to a different parking spot. As he turned the key, the engine made a horrible grinding sound and the car began to smoke huge billows of gray smoke from under the hood of the car. The smoke filled that area of the parking lot. The car simply would not start; it would not budge. I slid down into my seat, I'm sure very red-faced, and my husband was mortified to say the least. (Later, we found out from the mechanic that the starter he installed must have been faulty. The mechanic would replace it.), but it was too late for us. One by one, all the salesmen filed back into the building, snickering all the way. We were just left outside alone with a smoking car. It was like a bad script from a comedy movie. The car had to be towed out of the dealers and we had to be picked up by our daughter, who didn't find this amusing at all. When we got into our daughter's car, my husband and I broke into laughter – It was such a preposterous situation, you just had to laugh, and we did all the way home until our stomachs were hurting. Our teenage daughter didn't find it funny at all until years later! All that to say, we were without a car, we had no decent trade in, and we were short of money, plus a towing fee. I know it was God who helped us find humor in an otherwise very embarrassing situation.

Maybe you are someone who has suffered a great loss in your life, and it's very difficult for you to laugh or feel lighthearted in any way. Believe me, God understands, and cares about your pain. ***Psalm 147:3 says, "He heals the brokenhearted and binds up their wounds."***

Ask God to help you find humor in the little things in life even if you've suffered pain. Surround yourself around joyful people, instead of those who will feed your depression and pain. Pay attention to the programs on TV and the reading you are doing. Are they contributing to joy or depression? If the news on TV brings you down, then turn it off. You'd be surprised at how God will meet you and cause your heavy heart to lighten. ***Proverbs 15:13 says, "A*** *merry heart makes a cheerful countenance, but by sorrow of the heart, the spirit is broken." Proverbs 17:22 says, "A merry heart does good like medicine and a broken spirit dries the bones."*

I pray, my dear friend, that you would experience the lightheartedness and laughter of the Lord. It truly is good medicine and it doesn't cost a thing…

Websters Dictionary
Copyright 1967, G & C Merriam Co.
Pg. 477

Questions to Discuss

1. Do you experience laughter in your life?
2. Do you think you could be more lighthearted?
3. What do you think prevents you from having lightness of heart?
4. Do you think you take yourself too seriously? Can you easily laugh at yourself?
5. After reading this chapter, what are some practical steps you can take to help you to laugh more?

Notes

www.ingramcontent.com/pod-product-compliance
Ingram Content Group UK Ltd.
Pitfield, Milton Keynes, MK11 3LW, UK
UKHW041944230426
12048UKWH00008B/112